AWKWARD COMMUNICATION
Mastering Communication Through Life's Uncomfortable Moments

Joshua E. Bishop

Copyright © 2025 by Joshua E. Bishop

Printed in Houston, Texas, U.S.A.

All rights reserved. No part of this publication may be reproduced, distributed, or transmitted in any form without written permission from RWI Publishing House, P.O. Box 83, Ormond Beach, FL 32175. rwipublishing.com

RWI Publishing and RWI Publishing logo are registered trademarks of RWI Publishing House. Absence of (R) in connection with marks of RWI Publishing or other parties does not indicate an absence of registration of those marks.

Any refrence to historical events, real people, or real places are used with consent or fictitously. Names, characters and places are products of the author's imagination.

ISBN 979-8-9929274-0-5 (Paperback)
ISBN 979-8-9929274-1-2 (EPUB)

Library of Congress Control Number: 2025936517

Cover design by Charles Rivers
Cover photo by NEOSiAM 2024+/Pexels

First printing edition 2025.

RWI Publishing House
PO Box 83,
Ormond Beach, FL 32175
www.rwipublishing.com

For Sarah—

Your love has been my anchor, your care my comfort, and your support the quiet strength behind every page. Thank you for walking with me, believing in me, and encouraging me through every moment of this journey.

CONTENTS

SECTION ONE 1
Chapter 1: *It Starts With You* 3
Chapter 2: *The Gift of Awkwardness* ·····················9
Chapter 3: *The Power of Planning* 19
Chapter 4: *The Discipline of Practice* 27
Chapter 5: *The Need for Follow-Through* 33
Chapter 6: *The Cost of Communication* 39

SECTION TWO 45
Chapter 7: *Communication's Trivium* 47
Chapter 8: *The Trivium - Honesty* 51
Chapter 9: *The Trivium - Compassion* 59
Chapter 10: *The Trivium - Humility* 65
Chapter 11: *Read the Room* 73
Chapter 12: *Watch Your Step*..83
Conclusion 91

SECTION ONE

Welcome to the heart of this book—the part that holds the secret to transforming your communication. If you're looking for the "magic formula," the "aha moment," or the game-changing strategy that will truly elevate your ability to connect with others, you're about to find it right here.

I've intentionally cut out the fluff to bring you exactly what you need to get the most out of this book. No long-winded explanations or unnecessary tangents—just the essentials. This section is focused, concise, and practical, designed to give you the tools and insights you can start applying right away.

The truth is, effective communication isn't a mystery. It's a skill—one that can be learned and then mastered. And while there's no quick fix or shortcut, what you're about to dive into is the foundation that will reshape the way you communicate with the world. Think of this as the blueprint for success. These next few chapters will give you the tools, insights, and mindset shifts you need to stop just getting by in conversations and start truly thriving in them. So get ready—this is where the transformation begins.

CHAPTER ONE
IT STARTS WITH YOU

Communication is shaped by internal patterns —and those patterns can be changed.

You ever met someone who's just always in a good mood? The kind of person who seems to have rainbows and sunshine following them around, no matter what life throws at them? It's not just luck or magic dust. More often than not, these folks grew up in environments where positivity was a way of life. Maybe they had that one aunt who could turn every bad situation into an educational moment, or parents who made resilience and hope household values. These people who shine through life's storms are surely raised on grit and optimism.

But then, there's that one person whose positivity surprises you even more because they didn't have any of that. They didn't grow up in a warm, fuzzy environment. Maybe they had more emotional landmines than support systems, or their financial situation was one long battle. Yet, they're still optimistic. They've faced real hardships but somehow manage to keep that positive outlook. You can't help but wonder, "How on earth do they stay so upbeat despite everything?"

Here's the secret: *They changed their pattern of thinking.*

We're like sponges, soaking up the influences around us. From the moment we're born, every interaction leaves a mark on who we are. We might not even realize it, but those early relationships—our family, friends, teachers—lay the foundation for how we see the world and how we communicate within it. Over time, these influences become patterns that are reflected in our lives, and as we're about to dive into, they profoundly shape the way we communicate.

The real game-changer, though, is when someone decides to change those patterns. It's like upgrading the software that runs in the background of your mind. The thoughts and words that previously shaped them get a serious overhaul. Now, I'm not here to turn you into a relentless optimist—that's not what this book is about. This is about helping you recognize, embrace and overcome those awkward, uncomfortable feelings that often crop up in important conversations. However, as we'll see, the real key to becoming the best communicator is having the gumption to change your patterns.

The truth is, most of us don't realize how deeply rooted our communication patterns are. They've been programmed into us from the beginning—like a set of unspoken rules we follow without even thinking. For example, maybe you grew up in a family where disagreement was avoided at all costs, or perhaps you learned that showing vulnerability in a conversation was a sign of weakness. Those patterns shape how you approach conversations as an adult, often without you even being conscious of it.

What's fascinating is that these communication patterns aren't just taught at the dinner table. They're shaped by tons of things we don't even realize. Sure, there's the obvious stuff like your family, friends, and teachers, but what about those less obvious influences? Have you ever noticed how much a favorite TV show or movie shaped the way you interact? I remember watching The X-Files with my friends growing up. Now, I'm not out here trying to solve alien conspiracies, but

Mulder's calm, logical approach to the unknown and Scully's scientific skepticism might have made me think that being analytical and questioning was an admirable way to communicate. Those small influences, repeated over time, can seep into how you communicate without you even realizing it.

Then, there's social media. Oh, boy. If you've spent time scrolling through your feeds, you've definitely picked up patterns from there. It could be the way people argue—quick and snappy, leaving no room for nuance—or it could be the way we package our thoughts into catchy, shareable phrases that don't always leave space for depth or sincerity. What's worse, these patterns can influence not only how we speak to others but also how we hear what they're saying. The instant gratification of likes or shares on social media can make us crave immediate, concise responses in face-to-face conversations. Sometimes we're just trying to get our point across quickly because we've grown accustomed to 140 characters or less.

And here's a quirky one: Have you ever considered how your body posture influences your communication patterns? Think about the way you stand or sit when you're talking. Do you tend to cross your arms? Do you lean back or forward? Your body language is often a mirror of the unspoken patterns you've adopted over time. If you're the type of person who keeps your distance or folds your arms when you speak, it could be a learned pattern from growing up in environments where personal space or boundaries were highly valued—or maybe it's just a learned response from having your feelings dismissed in the past.

Even your friendships play a role in shaping communication patterns. If you've spent a lot of time around people who are open and vulnerable, you're likely to feel comfortable opening up in your conversations. But if you've been surrounded by people who keep their emotions locked up, you might struggle to express yourself in a more personal way. It's not just your family that shapes these patterns, but the network of people you surround yourself with—your friends, your coworkers, even acquaintances.

What's wild is that all of these little interactions and influences work together to create a mental blueprint for how we communicate. Some of these patterns are learned without us even knowing it. They just become the backdrop of our conversations, shaping our tone, body language, and even the words we choose. The key here is recognizing them. Once you can see these patterns, you can start to change them. Communication is a skill, and just like any other skill, it can be developed and improved with practice. The more we challenge and reshape our communication patterns, the better we become at navigating life's awkward moments and connecting with others.

CHAPTER TWO
THE GIFT OF AWKWARDNESS

Awkwardness signals a shift in communication patterns—and noticing those shifts helps you become a better communicator.

Our expectations and the way we interpret situations, including how we think a conversation might go wrong—are all shaped by patterns we've learned over time. Like our optimistic friend, we develop a kind of subconscious road-map that guides our communication.

These learned patterns influence everything, from our body language to those knee-jerk reactions that seem to come out of nowhere. In essence, these patterns mold our communication style and play a critical role in how we form and maintain relationships. Communication isn't just what you say, it's also what others hear, and these patterns shape both sides of that equation.

When I talk about communication patterns, I'm focusing on the ones we've learned over time—those habits and routines shaped by our experiences and interactions.

For example, think about how many of us were taught to always say "please" and "thank you." These simple phrases might seem like basic manners, but they're actually learned patterns of communication that we picked up from our parents, teachers, or even society.

There are also deeper patterns—the kind that feel almost programmed into our subconscious. Though these are learned behaviors as well, changing them often requires a great deal of self-reflection. They're important to recognize and work through because they tend to shape both our mood and our core behavior. The good news is, they can be addressed in a positive and healthy way.

While this book focuses more on practical tools for improving communication, the deeper work is done through the same process we'll use to become better communicators.

For now, let's focus on the patterns that more directly shape our communication—the ones that influence our words, our tone, and reactions. These are the patterns that impact how we connect with others in the everyday moments of life.

AWKWARDNESS INTRODUCED
When conversations feel awkward, it's usually because they don't follow our usual, comfortable patterns. Think about starting a new job. On day one, you're surrounded by people you've never met. You're used to the rhythm of conversations with your old team—everyone knew each other's inside jokes, quirks, and the jargon you've all created over time. Now, the usual patterns are just—missing. You don't know who likes dry humor, who gets frustrated by it, or what the unspoken rules of engagement are. Can you feel it? That tension in the air, where everyone's a little on edge, unsure of how to navigate this unfamiliar terrain? Even the most outgoing person can find themselves tongue-tied when the familiar patterns aren't there to lean on.

Recognizing that the pattern is off-kilter is the first step to fixing it. Just knowing that you're coloring outside the lines is often enough to start adapting. Really, just recognizing it can be enough to bring back a sense of normalcy. Well, I say recognition helps, but really it's accepting the fact that the pattern of communication has shifted.

We prolong the feeling of awkwardness when we sit back and wonder why we feel that way. By never putting our finger on what's happened, it only deepens the experience and can cause us to become paralyzed. Just knowing that the reason is due to a communication pattern-shift will help you quickly overcome those feelings and become a better communicator.

OBSERVATION
If you're wondering, "But how do I handle this?"—the answer is simple: observation. It's a tool you already have at your disposal. You've noticed the conversation has hit an awkward spot. You've sensed that continuing will make things uncomfortable for everyone. So while you've got the tool, the real issue might be that you're just not fully using it.

Observation demands more from you than just paying attention—but it does require that you pay attention. This is where awkwardness steps in as your greatest ally. Instead of seeing that awkwardness in conversation as a signal to run, train yourself to see it as a cue to start observing the situation and the discussion that's unfolding.

If you ask my family and closest friends, they'll tell you that I often say how much I love awkwardness. Why? Because it's a clear and wonderful red flag that the pattern of conversation has shifted. You've felt this before, haven't you? You're in a room with friends or colleagues, and there are three or four conversations happening all at once. Then, out of nowhere, all of them come to a natural end at the exact same moment. It's cosmic. It's ridiculously odd. And suddenly, everyone gets that funny look on their face like, "What just happened?"

That was the natural rhythm of all those different conversations finding their symmetrical end at the same time. That was a break in the pattern that everyone was comfortable with, or trying to stay comfortable with while in their own conversation. That moment is literally called an "awkward moment of silence." It happens in that sort of context as well as moments of group conversation when the flow from one subject to another just naturally comes to an end. My brother-in-law, David, hates that feeling so much that he picked up a habit to break the silence. When those moments happen, he'll just say, "What else?" It breaks the awkwardness and provides an opportunity for another round of conversation to begin.

When you feel that subtle twinge of awkwardness begin to creep up, you need to know that it's there to enhance your awareness of the situation. It's the "social flare" that's sent up so that you begin to observe more than just what's in front of you. This is when things get exciting.

You might think I'm crazy, but the first time awkwardness acts like a banner waving in the background of a conversation and you begin to observe the patterns shifting, your perception of awkwardness will begin to shift as well. It's like the rush of adrenaline right before the keynote speaker takes the stage. It's like the release of endorphins that kick in when an athlete takes the field with a cheering crowd. It heightens awareness and helps you engage on a totally different level.

"Ok...", you might say, "I've felt the awkwardness, I've recognized that it's a marker to start observing the communication that's taking place. What am I looking for?"

You're on the lookout for certain communication patterns, which I like to refer to as "dialects." These are the common ways people learn to communicate, much like learning a new language. Just as languages have unique accents that can make understanding difficult, communication dialects can create barriers between people in the same way. For instance, if you've ever heard someone speak in a Cockney or Essex accent, you know it can be challenging to follow. Even though they're speaking English, you might feel like you need a translator to fully grasp what they're saying.

The first step to becoming a great communicator is learning to be an excellent "dialect translator." In the rest of this chapter, I'll introduce you to a range of communication dialects, along with their key definitions. Don't worry if it feels like a lot at first. It might seem overwhelming, but I promise it's not as complicated as it looks. This list is here to show you the different ways people communicate—the different dialects. Once you can identify these dialects, you'll find it much easier to navigate and work with them than you might think.

To make things simpler, I've divided them into two basic categories.

EXPERIENTIAL	EMOTIONAL
Professional	Quiet
Familial	Angry
Personal	Conflict
Friendly	Excitement
Political	Coarse
Cunning	Relaxed
Informational	Manipulative

Professional: Those that recognize and respect the structure and hierarchy within an organization. When we engage in this type of communication, we're mindful of the established boundaries and roles, making sure to operate within them. At the same time, we keep our relationships at a professional distance, treating others more like acquaintances rather than close friends.

Familial: Share a similar respect for hierarchy but with a twist—they come with a layer of warmth and familiarity. In family settings, we might still recognize roles and structure, but there's an added closeness, a comfort that allows for more open and affectionate exchanges.

Personal: This dialect strips away much of the hierarchy you find in professional or familial settings. These are the conversations where warmth and familiarity take center stage, without the rigid structure or formal roles. It's the kind of communication that feels close and easygoing, where the focus is on the connection rather than any kind of established order.

Friendly: We could also call them, acquaintance communication patterns. These slide further down the spectrum. In these interactions, there's even less structure and warmth. These conversations tend to stay on the surface, with little emotional investment required from either party. It's more about casual exchanges where both the speaker and listener keep things light and at face value.

Political: This is all about persuasion and building support. These patterns may or may not involve manipulation, but the goal is clear: to gain trust and acceptance from others. Whether it's in a campaign speech or a business pitch, the communicator is focused on winning people over.

Cunning: Now, the notion of a "cunning dialect" might sound negative, but in the context of communication patterns, it's not necessarily a bad thing. Salespeople often use cunning patterns, carefully choosing their words to guide someone's thoughts and emotions in a specific direction. It's about being strategic with your communication to achieve a desired outcome.

Manipulative: Manipulative dialects however, take this a step further. These are used not just to share ideas and seek agreement but to actively steer people's beliefs and feelings toward what the communicator wants. It's less about mutual understanding and more about controlling the narrative.

Informational: These are straightforward and fact-driven. The goal is to convey data, details, and clarity, often without much emotional inflection. This style is efficient and organized, ensuring that the listener walks away with a clear understanding of the topic. It's particularly useful in professional or academic settings, where accuracy and precision are more important than emotional connection.

Quiet: This is a subtle and subdued dialect. In these exchanges, the speaker uses minimal words, often choosing to listen more than they speak. The tone is soft, and the message is delivered with restraint. This pattern often emphasizes thoughtfulness, allowing space for reflection and careful consideration of the other person's words, making it ideal for delicate situations where calmness is necessary.

Angry: Angry communication patterns are charged with emotion. These interactions are marked by raised voices, sharp tones, and a forceful delivery that often comes across as confrontational. The goal is less about understanding and more about expressing frustration or discontent. It's a pattern that can escalate tension quickly and often leaves little room for mutual resolution unless both parties are able to step back and de-escalate.

Conflict: These focus on addressing disagreement head-on. This style is direct and often urgent, seeking to clarify differences and resolve disputes. While it can be uncomfortable, conflict communication patterns are essential for bringing issues to the surface, as long as the focus remains on resolution rather than blame. If handled well, this pattern can lead to growth and deeper understanding between the parties involved.

Excitement: The excitement dialect pattern is energetic and enthusiastic. In these interactions, the speaker's tone is upbeat, their pace is quick, and their words are often punctuated with gestures or expressions that convey eagerness. This pattern is infectious, drawing others into the excitement and generating a sense of shared enthusiasm. It's the kind of communication that can inspire and motivate, but it can also overwhelm if the listener isn't on the same wavelength.

Coarse: These patterns are designed to alienate or divide. By creating a clear separation between groups of listeners, these patterns provoke strong emotions and reactions, whether the communicator is doing so intentionally or not. It's a way of drawing lines and pushing people into specific emotional or ideological camps.

Relaxed: These dialects are exactly as they sound, easygoing and laid-back. There's no rush, no urgency in these exchanges. The tone is casual, the words flow naturally, and the focus is more on maintaining a comfortable atmosphere than achieving any particular goal. It's a pattern where the conversation can meander, allowing for light-hearted banter and a sense of calm.

Manipulative: Finally, manipulative dialects are crafted to influence others, often by steering their thoughts or emotions in a specific direction. The speaker is strategic, using carefully chosen words, tones, and even non-verbal cues to guide the listener toward a desired outcome. While not always harmful, manipulative communication puts the speaker's goals ahead of mutual understanding, which can lead to a sense of mistrust or exploitation if the listener feels they're being controlled.

We come across all kinds of communication dialects depending on the situation and who we're talking to. In professional settings, for example, there's often a focus on structure and boundaries, while personal conversations let us be more open and emotionally connected. It's important to recognize which dialect is in play—whether it's one that's more strategic or persuasive, or one that's all about clarity, quiet reflection, or even resolving conflict. When we can spot these different styles, it helps us handle any conversation with more empathy, awareness, and purpose, making sure we stay thoughtful and effective, no matter what kind of interaction we're having.

CHAPTER THREE
THE POWER OF PLANNING

Effective communication doesn't happen by accident—it's cultivated through intention and clarity.

Recognizing Success
So, if the first step is recognizing the problem, the next step must be dealing with it, right? No.

Before tackling any of life's problems, you need to identify them but then believe in your ability to overcome them. Confidence in your ability to succeed is absolutely vital. Some people live their whole lives as pessimists, convinced that success is out of reach. For others, the idea of changing their life patterns seems downright impossible. If you've ever felt this way, I've got some great news for you— you're wrong.

Here's some advice that's helped me overcome this kind of thinking, and it's something I've applied in both my professional and personal life. It's a principle I've passed on to my wife, kids, and pretty much anyone who'll listen: You have to "make a plan and see it through." Now, here's where things usually go off the rails—either people fail to plan altogether, or they overthink the plan so much that they never actually move forward. Most fall into one of these two extremes: Failure to Plan or Analysis Paralysis.

You can make a plan, and you can see it through. If you're

You can make a plan, and you can see it through. If you're wondering whether you're capable of doing this, try a simple exercise. Grab a pencil or pen, and find one of the blank pages in this book. (If you're reading the e-book version, please don't write on your device!) Set a timer for five minutes. During those five minutes, jot down everything you need or want to do tomorrow—no particular order, just get it all down. Once you're sure you've listed everything, organize it by priority. Before the timer runs out, block out an hour of time for each item. If tomorrow isn't too busy, try it for an upcoming hectic day or plan for your week as a whole.

When it comes to tackling tasks or overcoming challenges, the key to success lies in creating a plan that's detailed enough to guide your steps, yet simple enough to prevent feeling overwhelmed. It's a delicate balance. Too vague, and you're left wandering aimlessly. Too complex, and you find yourself immobilized by the weight of details. The goal is to find the sweet spot between clarity and simplicity.

Once you've got your list ready, stick to that plan tomorrow. I guarantee that if you stay on task, it could be one of your most productive days in a long time. The key, though, is following through. Sure, things might pop up, and you'll have to adjust, but having a plan will help you refocus on the priorities you've set. If you see it through, you'll end the day with a renewed sense of confidence. You can make a plan, and you can absolutely follow through with it.

When it comes to recognizing dialects and implementing what's needed to be an effective communicator through "translation," having a plan is crucial. In the next section, we'll walk through exactly how to create that plan, tailored to your specific situation.

Make A Plan

Creating a plan to recognize and navigate communication dialects effectively involves a few universal principles that can guide anyone, regardless of the situation. Here are the key steps of your plan to help you become an effective "dialect translator" in any context:

D - Determine

Determine the environment and relationships before starting the conversation. Before diving in, assess the environment, the relationships involved, and the overall tone. Ask yourself: Is this a professional, personal, or casual interaction? Who am I speaking to, and what kind of outcome am I aiming for? This helps you recognize the most appropriate communication style or dialect before the first word is spoken.

I - Identify

Identify the communication style or dialect being used. Once you've assessed the situation, observe the communication patterns. Are you in a setting that calls for a professional, structured approach, or is it more relaxed and personal? Pay attention to verbal and non-verbal cues like tone, pacing, and formality. Identifying the dialect helps you understand how best to respond.

A - Attend (Attentive)

Attend to the conversation through active listening. Great communicators listen more than they speak. Focus on what the other person is expressing, not just with their words but also with their body language, tone, and pacing. Attending to these cues through active listening helps you adjust your response and build mutual understanding.

L - Listen

Listen with empathy and purpose. Communication is built on empathy and purpose. Recognizing the dialect goes beyond adjusting your language; it's about understanding where the other person is coming from emotionally and situationally. Keep their feelings, intentions, and needs in mind, always aiming for genuine understanding and connection.

E - Evaluate

Evaluate your approach and adapt your communication style. After identifying the dialect, adjust your approach to match or complement it. In a professional setting, use a structured, clear tone; in personal interactions, show warmth and openness. Align your communication style to the situation without losing sight of your intent.

C - Clarify

Clarify your objectives to guide your conversation. Before entering a conversation, know what you want to achieve. This doesn't need to be rigid, but a clear sense of direction helps guide your interaction. Ask: What message do I want to convey, and what do I hope the other person takes away? Clear objectives keep you focused, helping you adapt to different dialects effectively.

T - Translate

Translate the dialect to suit the context while staying true to your intent. As you adjust to the dialect being used, ensure your communication style suits the context. Whether professional or personal, maintain authenticity. Your goal is to translate the conversation into something that fosters understanding, while staying true to your objectives and maintaining clarity.

S - Self-Reflect
Self-reflect after the conversation to improve future interactions. After every significant conversation, take time to reflect. Did you recognize the dialect correctly? Were you able to adapt your communication style effectively? What could you have done differently? Reflecting on these elements allows you to continually improve as a communicator and better navigate future conversations.

Here's a simple way to think about these principles: they're tools you can use to plan your communication in any situation. The goal is to help you develop a personal approach to how you communicate. At first, it might feel awkward or forced, but as you practice, it will start to come naturally. Over time, you'll find yourself planning conversations without even realizing it.

Let's say you're preparing for a conversation with your boss about a potential promotion. You've been working hard, and this is the moment to express your goals and aspirations. Before you start speaking, let's break down how you could apply the D-I-A-L-E-C-T-S framework.

D - Determine the environment and relationships
First things first: what's the environment like? You're in a professional setting, and you know the tone will be formal. It's a one-on-one conversation with your boss, someone who holds a position of authority. Your relationship is professional, and you're aiming to make a clear, confident case for why you deserve this promotion. You can already tell that this will require a level of structure and professionalism in your communication.

I - Identify the communication style
Next, identify the communication style. You've noticed that

your boss appreciates clear, concise points—no fluff, no drama. You've observed that during meetings, he values directness, so you'll need to be straight to the point. There's a serious tone, but there's also openness, as he's been encouraging feedback and input from team members recently. This tells you it's important to be both professional and proactive.

A - Attend to the conversation through active listening
When you're speaking with your boss, you're not just talking. You're listening to his responses. Are his eyebrows furrowing when you mention certain accomplishments? Is he nodding when you bring up your key strengths? The non-verbal cues here matter just as much. Let's say he seems to be zoning out a little when you talk about your past projects. That's your cue to shift focus and explain how those projects tie into the promotion you're seeking, making sure to align with his priorities.

L - Listen with empathy and purpose
You're not only listening to words, but you're also paying attention to what's motivating your boss's response. Perhaps he's concerned about budget constraints or unsure of the next steps for the team. When you notice this, you adjust. You could say something like, "I understand the budget constraints, and I've thought about how I can add even more value without additional resources." This shows empathy toward his concerns while also keeping your conversation aligned with your purpose.

E - Evaluate your approach
Now, after a few minutes of discussing your goals, you realize that the tone is becoming a bit too formal for your usual work environment. Maybe you can lighten the mood a little to make the conversation flow more naturally. "I really

enjoy the challenges that come with this job. It's the kind of work that keeps me engaged, and I'd love to take on more responsibility." A shift like this can make the discussion feel less stiff and help it come across more naturally, while still staying professional.

C - Clarify your objectives
Before you even entered the room, you had a clear objective: express your interest in the promotion while showcasing your contributions and goals. As the conversation unfolds, keep that objective in mind. Don't get sidetracked by unnecessary details—stay focused on what you want to achieve. By articulating how you've contributed and how you envision your future role, you're making sure your intentions are crystal clear.

T - Translate the dialect to suit the context
Here, translating the dialect means taking your knowledge of your boss's communication style and adapting yours accordingly. He appreciates facts and figures, so you make sure to back up your points with specific data—whether it's revenue increases or team performance metrics. This translates your more personal aspirations into something he can relate to in terms of measurable results.

S - Self-reflect after the conversation
After the conversation, take a moment to reflect. Did you recognize the right dialect and adapt accordingly? Could you have been more concise in some areas? Was there a moment when you lost his attention, and what could you have done to regain it? By reflecting on these questions, you'll improve your approach for future conversations.

CHAPTER FOUR
THE DISCIPLINE OF PRACTICE

Growth in communication comes through consistent practice—not perfection.

Let's dive into the next and a significantly important step: *seeing it through.*

If you're someone who doesn't overthink or spend too much time planning, your challenge might lie in sticking with something until it's finished. It's not enough to simply start; you have to commit to following through. In my experience, the issue for most people isn't the inability to finish something—it's the struggle to get back on track when they've hit a roadblock or stumbled along the way—that is, when they've failed. You might think this is just a matter of semantics, but there's a big difference between not completing something and "failing" to follow through. One is an unfinished task; the other is a mindset.

Let me explain. When I set out to accomplish something and get interrupted—whether by distractions or unexpected obstacles—I sometimes feel like I've failed. That sense of failure can be overwhelming, even paralyzing. For some, the feeling of failure becomes motivation to try harder next time. But for most of us, moving past that feeling can be the hardest part. The truth is, pushing through those moments when you feel like you've failed is key to any kind of progress. You don't have to be Superman to do it, but you do need to learn how to move forward despite those setbacks.

Instead of seeing your efforts as a simple "pass" or "fail," start thinking of them as practice. Imagine practicing a piano piece at home—it's a lot different from performing it in front of a crowd at a recital, right? But many of us approach our daily challenges, especially conversations, as if we're always on stage, like every interaction is some high-stakes performance. When a conversation doesn't go the way you hoped, try to view it as just another practice session. Shifting your mindset this way can take the pressure off, making it easier to recover and try again.

That's really the key to being consistent: don't treat every attempt like it's do-or-die. Life isn't all-or-nothing; it's more like a series of stepping stones leading you forward. There's a quote often credited to Albert Einstein: "The reason for time is so that everything doesn't happen at once." In other words, time is just a sequence of events, one after the other. Yesterday's done, and what's in front of you is brand new. This mindset can help you let go of conversations or meetings that didn't go well last week. They weren't failures; they were lessons. The real question is, did you learn anything from them?

The bottom line is, you've got to believe in your ability to overcome. You have what it takes to succeed, but you have to recognize that in yourself. I could go on for pages, offering advice and strategies to improve communication, but none of it will make a difference if you don't believe in your own potential to grow and change. So, if you're already convinced that nothing can help and that change isn't possible, well, thanks for buying my book—but you might as well stop reading now.

...

If you're still with me, congratulations! You've already cleared the first hurdle—believing in yourself enough to give this whole communication thing a try. Now, let's keep moving forward.

When it comes to seeing a plan through—whether it's improving communication or tackling any other life goal—there are three key steps that can guide you toward success. These principles will help you stay focused, motivated, and resilient in the face of obstacles, even when it comes to obstacles in communication.

1. Commit to Consistency
Consistency is the backbone of seeing anything through. Improvement doesn't happen overnight; it's built through repeated effort over time. Whether you're refining a specific communication skill or working toward a larger life goal, make it a point to "show up" consistently. That doesn't mean perfection is required—there will be off days—but keeping yourself in the game, even with small daily efforts, ensures progress. Consistency builds momentum, and momentum keeps your plan alive.

2. Adapt and Persevere
No matter how well you plan, life rarely goes exactly as expected. When you hit roadblocks—and you will—be willing to adapt. Maybe a conversation didn't go as planned, or you struggled with a particular communication strategy. That's okay. The key is to evaluate what went wrong, make adjustments, and keep going. Perseverance isn't just about pushing through difficulties; it's about learning and evolving along the way. Successful follow-through depends on your ability to stay flexible while maintaining your commitment to the end goal.

3. Personal Accountability

Accountability is key to follow-through. Set personal goals for each conversation—whether it's practicing better listening, asking more thoughtful questions, or handling conflict more calmly. Afterward, check in with yourself to see if you met those goals. By holding yourself accountable for improving specific communication skills, you create a clear path to becoming a more effective communicator over time.

My wife, Sarah, once told me something that has stuck with me: "*Time will pass regardless, so you might as well put in the effort.*" When you take that approach, there's only one direction to go—forward. If you're anything like me, you've probably had moments where the momentum just fizzled out. Maybe you started strong with a plan, but the details became overwhelming. Or maybe you faced some setbacks, and suddenly it felt easier to just stop than to keep pushing forward. But here's the key—growth doesn't happen in bursts of excitement; it happens in small, steady steps, day after day. If you're consistent, even on the hard days, you'll see progress.

The best part? You're capable of doing this. The only difference between someone who accomplishes their goals and someone who doesn't is the willingness to see it through. The hard days? They're a given. The real question is: Will you keep showing up, even when it feels difficult or when the end seems far off? You have everything you need to succeed; it's just a matter of trusting in your ability to push through and take that next step. If you take this approach—if you decide to stay committed to the effort, no matter the obstacles—you'll find that the path forward isn't just possible; it's inevitable. You can make this a habit. You can see it through. And over time, the little steps you take will add up to something much bigger than you ever imagined.

CHAPTER FIVE
THE NEED FOR FOLLOW-THROUGH

The key to better connection is learning to lean into the moment, not away from it.

We've already discussed how to move past the awkwardness that comes with unfamiliar patterns by learning to recognize and embrace them. With practice, these patterns start to feel more natural, and once you take that first step, the hardest part is behind you.

Now, it's time to take it a step further. Now we want to explore how we can confidently lean into these new patterns, making the "*lean*" a natural part of your communication style.

Imagine you're trying to learn to dance. At first, you're going to feel ridiculous, tripping over your own feet, maybe even stepping on your partner's toes. But the more you practice, the more natural those steps will become. You'll go from counting in your head, "One, two, three, four," to just moving with the music. That's how it works with new communication patterns too. Let me give you a simple example to show what I mean.

Let's say you're having a friendly conversation with a coworker, and suddenly the tone shifts to a more professional one. What just happened? Chances are you've experienced this before—maybe the boss walked in, and your co-worker wants to avoid getting in trouble for chatting during work hours. There's usually a good reason for an abrupt change in communication like that. Whether or not there is, the best thing you can do in that moment is quickly adjust your approach to match the new tone. That's what I call "*leaning into the awkward.*"

You already do this. You naturally adapt to different communication patterns without even realizing it. If you've been in a situation like the one described, the awkwardness has likely faded over time. Sure, there might still be a brief moment of discomfort, but you've learned to handle the shift and "*embrace it.*" That's why I'm confident that all you really need is a better understanding of what's happening.

The example I gave is probably familiar to you, and as soon as you read it, you likely thought, "Oh, the boss just walked in." That's exactly why I use it—it shows that you can handle these shifts. You just need to get comfortable with the different communication patterns you and others use. When those patterns change, it's all about embracing the shift and learning to roll with it.

Five Simple Steps

We're familiar with the different "conversation dialects" we use, so let's take the next step and figure out how to embrace those awkward moments when things don't go quite as expected. We've all been there—a casual chat suddenly feels tense, or a friendly conversation turns serious. Instead of avoiding it, these moments are actually opportunities for growth. Here are five practical ways to lean into the awkwardness when it happens.

1. Acknowledge the Shift
The first and most universally useful way to manage an awkward moment is to simply acknowledge it. When a conversation shifts unexpectedly—whether due to a new

person joining or a topic change—addressing the shift can ease the tension. You could say something like, "It feels like the conversation has taken a turn, has anyone else noticed?" or "Let's recognize that something feels different now." By doing this, you show awareness of the change and help others feel more at ease. If you've noticed it, chances are others have as well.

2. Practice Patience and Pause
When things get uncomfortable, our instinct is often to fill the silence or rush through it. However, sometimes the best move is to pause, take a breath, and let the moment settle. A brief pause gives everyone time to think and helps prevent reacting too quickly. It also signals that you're confident and in control of the situation. A simple pause can transform a potentially awkward moment into a more thoughtful, balanced exchange.

3. Stay Curious
Awkwardness often arises from not knowing how to proceed or when a conversation veers into unfamiliar territory. The best way to handle this is to stay curious. Instead of backing away from the discomfort, ask open-ended questions. Curiosity can transform an awkward pause into an opportunity for deeper conversation. For example, if someone brings up a sensitive topic, you could say, "That's interesting—can you tell me more about what you're thinking?" This shows you're willing to dive in and learn, even when the conversation feels a little uncomfortable.

4. Use Humor (But Gently)
Humor can be a great way to break the tension, but it's important to use it carefully. A light joke or self-deprecating comment can ease the pressure, but you should avoid undermining the seriousness of the situation. For example, if

the conversation suddenly feels formal or tense, you might smile and say, "Wow, we just shifted gears, didn't we?" This allows everyone to laugh without making anyone feel uncomfortable or minimizing the moment.

5. Be Vulnerable

Sometimes, the best way to embrace awkwardness is to simply admit it. Acknowledging your own discomfort can actually help put others at ease. If the conversation is moving into unfamiliar or difficult territory, you might say something like, "I'm not exactly sure where to go from here, but I'm glad we're having this conversation." This honesty shows that you're willing to engage even when it's tough, encouraging others to do the same and deepening the connection.

By using these five strategies, you can turn awkward moments into opportunities for connection and growth. Instead of dreading those times when the conversation takes an unexpected turn, you can embrace them and use them to become a more confident and effective communicator.

CHAPTER SIX
THE COST OF COMMUNICATION

Effective communication requires courage, clarity, and a willingness to face the consequences.

Let's take a moment to talk about what happens after the conversation—the aftermath. This isn't your cue to avoid it or walk away, but a chance to pause and reflect on what's at stake. We must recognize the cost of communication and the impact our words can have.

Often, it's the hesitation to confront awkwardness that holds us back from saying what truly needs to be said. Yet, this hesitation also serves as a reminder to choose our words wisely when we decide to speak honestly. It acts like a pressure valve, releasing just enough tension to prevent us from blurting out something we might later regret.

We've all experienced that tipping point—maybe it's after a coworker's snarky remark or your spouse's sigh of frustration that finally pushes you over the edge. Chances are, there were moments earlier when you held back, when something needed to be said, but you stayed silent to avoid the discomfort. But after that moment of snapping, doesn't the situation become even more awkward and strained?

This is where things often break down. Being overly mindful of potential outcomes can paralyze us and stop communication in its tracks. We become so afraid of hurting the people we care about or those we work with that we say nothing at all. But here's the truth: fear is a terrible motivator. Fear of rejection, fear of judgment, fear of failure—these things block progress. In communication, as in life, fear can't be allowed to stop us from moving forward.

It's important to acknowledge that awkward conversations might not always go smoothly. Being honest might strain relationships or cause discomfort. But if we take the time to weigh the cost of staying silent versus speaking up, we often realize that adopting a new communication pattern is worth the risk. Sometimes, the consequences of saying nothing are far worse.

I once heard a quote: "We're not stressed because of what we do, but because of what we refuse to do." People rarely lose their temper over the first issue that comes up. More often, they snap after ignoring important things for too long. This isn't just about keeping your composure; it's about recognizing that avoiding critical conversations comes with its own set of consequences.

There's always a price to pay for being honest and upfront, but there's also a price for neglecting communication. Striking a balance is key, but more often than not, we tip too far in one direction—either saying too much too harshly or avoiding the conversation altogether.

By considering the potential outcomes of a conversation, you don't just regulate your words and tone—you also begin to develop a more thoughtful communication pattern. This awareness helps you break free from the cycle of avoidance that often leads to snapping or feeling overwhelmed. You'll start to recognize when it's time to speak up, even if it feels uncomfortable. The key isn't just managing these conversations, but reshaping how you approach them altogether.

I won't give you a script for every situation—that's something you'll discover through experience. But the first step is learning to step outside your usual habits. Just as ignoring the need for communication can build unnecessary stress, addressing issues early can prevent that buildup. Embrace the challenge of handling these moments differently, and you'll develop a communication style that works for you, even in the most awkward of situations.

Here are four simple steps for evaluating when to hold back from speaking, as well as four steps for knowing when it's the right time to speak up.

Four Questions Before You Speak:

1. Assess the Emotional Climate: Before saying anything, take a moment to gauge the emotional temperature of the conversation. Are people upset, defensive, or frustrated? If emotions are running high, it might be better to hold off until things have calmed down.

2. Consider Long-Term Impact: Ask yourself, "Will this comment help or harm the relationship in the long run?" If your words are likely to create more harm than good, it's a sign to pause.

3. Reflect on Your Motive: What is driving your desire to speak? Is it frustration, anger, or the need to prove a point? If your motive is emotionally charged or self-serving, it may be best to hold back until you can approach the conversation with more clarity.

4. Weigh the Necessity: Is what you're about to say essential to the situation, or can it wait? Sometimes, the thing you feel

needs to be said might not be as urgent as it seems. If waiting could lead to a more productive conversation later, silence might be your best option.

Four Signs It's Time to Speak:

1. **When Silence Could Cause Harm:** If avoiding the conversation could lead to misunderstandings, resentment, or further complications, it's time to speak. Holding back can often make things worse over time.

2. **If the Issue is Recurrent:** If the same problem keeps surfacing and it hasn't been addressed, it's a sign that you need to speak up. Unresolved issues rarely go away on their own and tend to create ongoing tension.

3. **When Your Input is Valuable:** If your perspective or insight could contribute positively to the conversation or bring about a solution, then it's the right time to share. Speaking up when you have something constructive to offer is essential for progress.

4. **When Timing is Right:** Look for a moment when the emotional climate is calm, and the other person is likely to be more receptive. If the atmosphere feels open to conversation, it's a good opportunity to express what needs to be said.

These steps help balance the consideration of consequences with the importance of honest communication, guiding you on when to hold back and when to lean in. Let's look at an example to bring more clarity.

You've been working with Jane on a big project, but she keeps missing deadlines, and it's starting to affect the team.

She hands in another late report today, and you're fed up. Before reacting, let's go through a few steps to decide how to approach the situation.

Four Questions Before You Speak:
1. Emotional Climate:
Jane looks stressed and overwhelmed. It's probably not the best time to confront her right now.

2. Long-Term Impact:
If you bring it up angrily, it could hurt your relationship. But if you don't speak up, the issue will keep growing. You need to find the right moment.

3. Your Motive:
Are you just venting, or do you really want to solve the problem? You realize it's more about getting things back on track, not just venting your frustration.

4. Necessity:
The issue needs to be addressed, but waiting for a calmer time might help the conversation go better.

Four Signs It's Time to Speak:
1. Silence Could Cause Harm:
If you don't say anything, the problem will continue and might cause more issues later.

2. It's a Recurrent Issue:
This isn't the first time, so it needs to be addressed now.

3. Your Input is Valuable:
You have ideas to help Jane manage her deadlines, and your feedback could improve the situation.

4. Timing:
The office has quieted down, and Jane seems calmer. Now's the right time to bring it up.

SECTION TWO

Section Two is where the philosophy of communication transforms into a practical guide for mastering your conversations. While Section One gave you the secret to communication—the foundational skills to start improving right away—this section dives deeper into the "why" behind it all. It's not just about knowing the right techniques, but understanding the principles that truly shape how we communicate.

In these chapters, we'll focus on three essential elements: honesty, compassion, and humility. These are the core philosophies that can help you break through any awkwardness you might feel and build stronger connections in every conversation. By understanding and embracing these principles, you'll be equipped to approach every interaction with more confidence and authenticity.

This section is about more than just practical tips. It's about embracing the heart of communication—how we communicate with others, and how we communicate with ourselves. By the end, you'll not only have the tools to navigate conversations more effectively, but also a deeper understanding of why those tools matter and how to implement them in your daily life. So, take a deep breath, dive in, and get ready to rethink the way you approach every conversation.

CHAPTER SEVEN
COMMUNICATION'S TRIVIUM

Great communication is built on a foundation of honesty, shaped by compassion, and held together by humility.

In Latin, trivium means "meeting of three ways." In classical education, it referred to grammar, rhetoric, and logic—the foundational disciplines for all higher learning. Ancient educators believed that before a person could master philosophy or science, they first had to master how to think, speak, and understand.

The trivium wasn't just a curriculum—it was a way of forming people. It taught them how to process truth, express it clearly, and engage others in meaningful discourse. While the early Greeks laid the groundwork, it was the medieval educators who formalized the trivium as the essential path to wisdom.

In that spirit, I'm borrowing the term here—not to give you a history lesson, but to show how three essential elements must also meet in your communication: honesty, compassion, and humility. These aren't academic categories—they're practical tools, and they form a kind of internal compass for navigating conversations with both clarity and character.

Communication isn't just about what we say—it's about what others actually hear. Anyone can talk, but real communication requires more than words; it demands presence, discernment, and intention. Plato once said that wise speech must "aim at the soul." That's the heart of communication—it's not merely transferring data, it's transmitting meaning, emotion, and understanding. That's why effort alone isn't enough.

You can be articulate and still be misunderstood. You can speak with confidence and still leave people feeling unheard. The goal isn't just to express yourself—it's to connect. And for that to happen, your words must carry the weight of honesty, the warmth of compassion, and the posture of humility. These three virtues don't just shape what you say—they shape how you're received.

Think of it like building a house: you start with a foundation, then raise the walls, and finally secure the roof. Each part is essential, but none stand alone. Without a solid foundation, the structure collapses. Without walls, there's nothing to support it. Without a roof, everything inside is exposed and vulnerable.

In the same way, communication needs all three—honesty as the foundation, compassion as the framing that gives form and strength, and humility as the covering that keeps everything grounded, secure, and above all—human. Remove one, and the whole structure weakens. But when they work together, they create conversations that are not only clear but deeply meaningful. That's the kind of communication we should strive for.

CHAPTER EIGHT
THE TRIVIUM - HONESTY

Honest communication begins with self-awareness and grows through the courage to speak truthfully with both clarity and care.

The Foundation

Honesty is more than just telling the truth—it's the foundation of clear communication. When we think of honesty, we often focus on avoiding lies, but in reality, honesty plays a much broader role in shaping how we interact with others. It's about authenticity, trust, and openness, and it plays a crucial part in how we relate to people, both personally and professionally.

Honesty starts with a willingness to be open about who we are, what we believe, and how we feel. It requires self-reflection and a commitment to speaking truthfully, even when it might be uncomfortable. In communication, this goes beyond just avoiding deceit. It means presenting information in a way that is both truthful and considerate of the listener. While honesty should always be grounded in facts, it also takes into account the relational aspect of communication—how your words affect the other person and what they mean within the context of your relationship.

2D Honesty

Honesty in communication can be broken down into two main dimensions: the content dimension and the relationship dimension. The content dimension refers to the factual information shared in a message. For example, if you're asked for feedback at work or in a personal relationship, the content is your direct response—whether you think a project was successful or how you feel about a certain issue. This aspect of honesty is relatively straightforward, but it's only one piece of the puzzle.

The relationship dimension is just as, if not more, important. This is where the nuance of honesty truly comes into play. It's not just about what you say, but how you say it and what your words convey about your relationship with the other person. This dimension involves the unspoken message behind the content—the tone, timing, and the emotions you express. For example, sharing honest feedback with a colleague in a way that respects their feelings and encourages growth differs greatly from bluntly offering criticism without regard for their emotions. While both may communicate the same factual information, the relational impact is entirely different.

This balance between truthfulness and consideration for the other person is where honesty transcends being merely an ethical rule; it becomes a skill that strengthens relationships.

Relational Honesty
Honesty builds trust, and trust is the bedrock of any healthy relationship. When you are honest with someone, you allow them to see who you really are, and that vulnerability invites closeness. It shows the other person that you trust them with your true thoughts and feelings, and in return, it encourages them to do the same. Over time, this mutual openness deepens the relationship and creates a sense of security that's difficult to break.

However, honesty in relationships isn't just about "not lying." It's about fostering an environment where both people feel safe to express their true selves. In practice, this might look like sharing your feelings about a difficult situation or admitting when you've made a mistake. It's about being real with each other, even when it feels uncomfortable.

But there's a fine line between being honest and being hurtful. Not every thought or opinion needs to be shared at every moment. Honesty is not an excuse for being critical or insensitive. It requires discernment—knowing when to speak up and when to hold back. This doesn't mean withholding important information; rather, it's about choosing the right time and manner to present the truth in a way that's both constructive and kind.

For example, if your partner asks for feedback on something important to them, you can be honest without being harsh. Instead of merely pointing out what's wrong, you can frame your feedback in a way that acknowledges their effort and offers constructive suggestions. This kind of honesty doesn't just communicate the facts; it shows that you care about their feelings and their growth.

Professional Honesty
Workplace environments thrive on trust and transparency, and being honest with colleagues and supervisors helps create a culture of openness. This fosters collaboration, sparks innovation, and ensures problems are addressed before they escalate.

For instance, if you're working on a team and notice a project is going off track, being honest about your concerns can help prevent bigger issues later. It might feel awkward to speak up, especially if your opinion isn't popular, but doing so shows integrity and a commitment to the team's success. Similarly, being honest with your boss about challenges you're facing can lead to better support and resources, making it easier to achieve your goals.

That said, honesty in the workplace also requires tact. Just like in personal relationships, the way you deliver your message matters. Offering feedback to a colleague in a respectful and solution-oriented way is far more effective than simply pointing out what's wrong. This type of honesty strengthens working relationships and makes it easier for everyone to collaborate toward common goals.

Personal Honesty
In personal relationships, honesty is just as crucial, but it often takes on a more emotional role. Whether with family or friends, being open and honest builds trust, which is the foundation of any strong relationship. It's not just about telling the truth when it's convenient—true honesty involves being vulnerable and expressing your feelings, even when it's uncomfortable.

For example, imagine you're feeling overwhelmed by a friend who constantly leans on you for support but doesn't seem to realize you're struggling with your own issues. You could stay quiet to avoid an awkward conversation, but being honest about your feelings will benefit the relationship in the long run. You might say something like, "I value our friendship, but lately I've been feeling a bit overwhelmed, and I need to take a step back to focus on my own well-being." It's a tough conversation to have, but sharing how you feel prevents resentment from building up and opens the door for a more balanced, healthy relationship.

Of course, honesty in personal relationships also requires kindness. It's not just about what you say, but how you say it. If your goal is to strengthen the relationship, it's important to approach these conversations with empathy and a willingness to listen. This kind of honesty creates deeper connections and fosters an environment where both people feel understood and respected.

Growing Honesty:
The first step in growing in the area of honesty in your communication is to develop a sense of self-awareness. Honest communication begins with knowing your own thoughts and feelings clearly so you can express them accurately. This means taking the time to reflect on your emotions and the reasons behind them before engaging in conversation. Personal reflection, journaling, or even discussing things with a trusted friend can help you practice articulating your thoughts more precisely. The more you understand your own mind, the easier it will be to communicate your thoughts clearly and confidently.

Another key aspect is practicing honesty in small, everyday interactions, which builds your comfort level in being direct without being abrasive. Instead of avoiding difficult topics or softening your stance too much to keep the peace, get used to expressing yourself authentically but kindly.

Another important part of improving honest communication is learning to balance transparency with tact. It's not enough to simply tell the truth; you must also be mindful of how that truth is received. Start by considering the other person's perspective—ask yourself how they might interpret your words and how you can deliver your message in a way that is honest but also empathetic.

One helpful approach is to frame honesty in terms of mutual benefit. For example, instead of focusing on just getting something off your chest, approach the conversation with a mindset that aims to build understanding and strengthen the relationship. If a colleague has been missing deadlines and it's affecting your workload, rather than saying, "You're always late with your tasks, and it's frustrating," you could say, "I've noticed some delays recently, and it's made it harder to keep things on track. Can we figure out how to improve the process so we both stay on schedule?" This keeps the focus on solving the problem together, rather than just expressing frustration.

There's an important point to address here: the risk of using this approach to manipulate others. The goal isn't to "handle" anyone—it's to enhance your ability to communicate honestly while keeping the conversation open. A big part of that is truly listening to the other person.

Active listening is key here. Communication isn't just about what you say; it's also about how well you listen. When you take the time to hear and acknowledge the other person's response, you create space for honest conversation that builds trust and goodwill.

By being a good listener, you not only avoid "handling" people, but you also show them that your words are about genuinely caring how they understand you.

CHAPTER NINE
THE TRIVIUM - COMPASSION

Compassionate communication begins when we stop speaking to be heard and start listening to understand—connecting not just with words, but with heart.

Compassion is what makes our interactions truly human. It's more than just understanding someone else's feelings—it's about feeling those emotions with them and responding in a way that lifts them up. Compassion, or empathy, is what turns understanding into action. When we're compassionate, we're not just hearing the other person—we're connecting with their emotions and responding with care and kindness.

The Heart

No matter who you're speaking with, communication is about connecting with their heart, not just their face. It's about reaching beyond words and engaging with their emotions. At its core, compassion is about connection. It allows us to step outside of ourselves and see the world from another person's perspective. This is especially important in communication because it shifts our focus from what we want to say to what the other person needs to hear. Compassion helps us be better listeners, more patient communicators, and more thoughtful in our responses.

Compassion vs. Empathy

Before diving deeper, it's important to clarify the distinction between empathy and compassion, as the two are often confused. Empathy is the ability to understand and feel what someone else is experiencing. It's an essential step toward compassion, but it's not the full picture. Empathy allows us to relate to another person, but compassion takes it a step further by motivating us to take action—whether that action is offering comfort, helping to solve a problem, or simply being present for someone in their time of need.

For example, if a colleague shares that they're struggling with a personal issue, empathy allows you to understand and feel their pain. Compassion, however, drives you to offer support, whether through words of encouragement, offering to help with their workload, or simply being a listening ear. Compassion is active, not passive, and it turns empathy into something tangible.

Active Listening

One of the most effective ways to show compassion in communication is through active listening. Active listening is about more than just hearing words; it's about fully engaging with the speaker, showing that you're invested in what they're saying, and responding thoughtfully. When we actively listen, we're not waiting for our turn to speak or thinking about our response while the other person is talking. Instead, we're fully focused on understanding their message and the emotions behind it.

Active listening can be demonstrated in simple but powerful ways: by nodding in agreement, maintaining eye contact, and providing verbal cues like "I see" or "That makes sense." Repeating back what you've heard to confirm understanding is another excellent technique. For instance, saying, "So what

I'm hearing is that you're feeling overwhelmed because of the deadlines," not only confirms that you've understood the message but also shows that you're attuned to the emotional undercurrent of what's being said.

In both personal and professional settings, active listening is a vital component of compassionate communication. It shows the other person that you value their perspective and are fully present in the conversation, building trust and fostering a deeper connection.

Be careful, though. Many people teach active listening as a tactic to get ahead, but just nodding and repeating words isn't the same as truly listening. One is a manipulative tool, while real active listening is about genuinely understanding the other person's perspective and intentions.

Relational Compassion

Personal Compassion
In personal relationships, compassion is what strengthens real connections. It's about showing up for the other person, not just when things are going well, but also when they're stressed, scared, or hurting. Compassion doesn't always look the same—sometimes it means offering helpful advice, and other times it's simply being there to listen or offer comfort. The key is ensuring that the other person feels truly seen and supported, no matter how that support is expressed.

For example, if a friend confides in you about a difficult decision they're facing, your first instinct might be to offer advice or try to solve the problem. However, the most compassionate response is often simply to listen. By giving them the space to express their emotions without judgment or rushing to provide solutions, you show that you care and that their feelings matter. Compassion isn't about having all the answers; it's about creating a safe space for the other person to be vulnerable.

Compassion also plays a role in navigating conflict. In any relationship, disagreements are bound to happen, but how we handle them can make all the difference. Approaching conflict with compassion means trying to understand where the other person is coming from, rather than immediately jumping to defend your position. It means giving them the benefit of the doubt and seeking to resolve the issue in a way that honors both your needs and theirs. Compassion softens the edges of tough conversations and makes it easier to find common ground.

Being quick to hear and slow to speak is tough, and honestly, you'll mess up sometimes. But don't be discouraged—it's a skill that takes time and practice to develop. I once told a friend, "Practice makes perfect," and he corrected me, saying, "Practice makes permanent, not perfect." That small shift in thinking is important because it changes what you expect from yourself, even after years of practice. So, keep practicing patience with people. Let real care and compassion guide you, and remember that no matter how long you've been at it, you'll never be perfect— just steadily better.

Professional Compassion
In the workplace, compassion is often overlooked in favor of efficiency and results. But the truth is, compassionate communication can boost productivity and create a more positive work environment. When colleagues feel supported and understood, they're more likely to collaborate effectively, manage stress better, and stay motivated.

Compassionate leadership, in particular, is a powerful tool. Leaders who show compassion—by listening to their team, offering support when needed, and being understanding of challenges—build stronger, more loyal teams. For instance, if an employee is struggling to meet a deadline due to personal issues, a compassionate leader might offer flexibility or reassign tasks to ease the burden. This not only relieves immediate stress but also shows the employee they're valued as a person, not just a worker.

Compassionate communication in professional settings also means being mindful of how feedback is delivered. Instead of focusing only on what's wrong, compassionate feedback recognizes effort and offers suggestions for improvement. This approach not only encourages growth but also strengthens relationships between colleagues—or between a manager and their team.

Growing Compassion

Compassion isn't something that just happens—it's a skill you can develop with practice. One way to grow in compassion is through mindfulness. Taking a moment to pause and consider the other person's feelings before responding can make a meaningful difference in how your message is received. It helps you approach the conversation with a clearer perspective and deeper empathy.

Ultimately, compassion in communication is about building real connection and understanding. Whether in personal relationships or professional settings, approaching conversations with compassion creates deeper, more meaningful interactions—and often leads to better outcomes for everyone involved.

CHAPTER TEN
THE TRIVIUM - HUMILITY

Humility transforms communication by quieting the ego, opening space for growth, and creating connection through teachability and grace.

Quiet Strength

Humility is often misunderstood as weakness or self-doubt, but in reality, it's a powerful tool for communication. It's about recognizing that we don't have all the answers and staying open to learning from others. In conversation, humility creates space for understanding and collaboration. It helps us approach dialogue with curiosity instead of judgment—making our interactions more thoughtful, respectful, and effective.

Humility is one of the strongest displays of self-control you can show. It's about striking the right balance between confidence and openness—being able to take feedback without getting defensive. Humility is a true mark of strength. Nothing frustrates an angry person more than having their rant met with calm, confident acceptance of fair criticism, while gently brushing aside anything over-the-top or unfair. It's the quiet power of staying grounded, even in the middle of someone else's storm.

Bold Humility

Humility is the combination of honesty and courage. There's a common misunderstanding about what humility really means. Many people assume that being humble is the same as being weak or timid. But true humility isn't the opposite of strength. Real humility is about being bold in the right way—it's about standing strong while also having an honest understanding of your own limits.

Some think bravery is all about digging in your heels and refusing to budge. But boldness without self-awareness isn't boldness at all—it's arrogance, and there's nothing admirable about that. True courage comes from understanding what's really happening and making decisions based on what's right. If life is the most valuable thing, for instance, a brave soldier doesn't hesitate to rush into danger to save others. That's real courage—seeing the risk and choosing to do what needs to be done anyway.

Humility, at its core, is about being honest with yourself about what you know and what you can do—and then having the courage to take the right action. It's not about shrinking back; it's about stepping up in the right way, with a clear view of who you are and what's needed.

On the battlefield of communication, honesty keeps boldness from becoming overbearing. It reminds us that no matter how strongly we feel about our opinions, there's always room to hear other perspectives. In fact, the ability to listen to and reflect on feedback without taking it personally is one of the greatest strengths a communicator can develop. This balance is especially important in settings where collaboration matters—like teams or partnerships—because it opens the door for better ideas and stronger relationships.

Humility in Personal Relationships

In personal relationships, humility can be the difference between productive conversations and ongoing conflict. When we're humble, we approach conversations with a willingness to understand the other person's perspective instead of just trying to prove we're right. That doesn't mean ignoring your own thoughts or feelings—it simply means recognizing that you might not have the full picture and that the other person's view is worth hearing.

For example, in a disagreement with a spouse or friend, humility allows you to say, "I might not see the whole story here," or "Help me understand your side of things." That kind of mindset shifts the conversation from winning an argument to finding common ground. It invites collaboration instead of competition.

Humility also helps diffuse tension during conflict. By acknowledging your own role in a disagreement and staying open to compromise, you create an environment where both people feel heard and respected. A simple "I could be wrong" or "I'm open to hearing your thoughts" can go a long way in resolving issues in a healthy way. That kind of openness invites both sides to come together and find a solution, instead of digging in and getting stuck in a cycle of blame.

Humility in Professional Settings

In the workplace, humility is just as important. Professional environments thrive on collaboration, problem-solving, and feedback—and humility is key to navigating all three. It encourages people to admit when they don't have all the answers, ask for help when needed, and stay open to learning from others. At its core, humility creates a culture of growth and improvement. It says, "I'm always learning— so show me what I don't know."

For example, a team leader who's humble enough to accept feedback from their team fosters an environment where everyone feels valued. Instead of leading with an iron fist, they lead by example—demonstrating that even those in charge don't have all the answers and can benefit from the insights of others. This kind of leadership encourages team members to speak up, share ideas, and offer constructive feedback, knowing their input is respected and genuinely appreciated.

Humility also plays a crucial role in how we handle mistakes in the workplace. Confidence and collaboration thrive in an environment where people—whether employees or managers—own their mistakes and take responsibility, rather than shifting blame or making excuses. That kind of accountability builds trust across the team and sets the tone for how challenges and setbacks are handled. When team members see their leaders or colleagues admit fault and take steps to improve, it creates a culture of courage and reminds everyone that their value isn't tied to always being right.

Humble Listening
Perhaps the most important aspect of humility in communication is the ability to listen without judgment. When we're truly humble, we recognize that everyone has something to teach us, and we approach conversations with curiosity instead of assumption. That means listening not just to respond, but to genuinely understand. I've said this time and time again—and that just shows how vital this really is. It's about asking thoughtful questions, seeking clarity, and staying open to ideas that might challenge your own.

Listening with humility means recognizing that you don't always know best. It takes setting aside your ego and being willing to learn from others, even when their perspective challenges your own. This is especially important in professional environments, where collaboration and teamwork drive success. When you listen with humility, you create space for fresh ideas and honest dialogue, which leads to better solutions and stronger relationships.

Growing Humility

Humility doesn't always come naturally, but it can be developed with practice. One way to cultivate it is by regularly reflecting on your own communication habits. Are you quick to jump in with your opinion, or do you take time to truly listen? Do you approach conversations with an open mind, or are you more focused on proving your point?

A helpful practice is to pause before responding in conversations. That brief moment gives you space to consider whether you're truly listening or just waiting for your turn to talk. It also helps you check in with yourself—are you approaching the conversation with humility, or are you letting your ego take the lead?

Another way to practice humility is to actively seek feedback from others. Ask for input on your communication style, and stay open to what they have to say. It might feel uncomfortable at first, but it's a powerful way to grow. The more receptive you are to feedback, the more you'll learn about yourself—and the better you'll become at improving your interactions with others.

Ultimately, humility in communication means recognizing that we all have room to grow. Whether in personal relationships or professional settings, approaching conversations with humility creates space for collaboration, learning, and connection. It helps us listen more deeply, speak more thoughtfully, and build stronger, more respectful relationships.

By embracing humility, we open the door to more meaningful conversations and help create a culture of trust and openness. In doing so, we grow into better communicators, stronger collaborators, and more grounded, impactful people.

Conclusion

Honesty is the foundation of all communication, rooted in truthfulness and transparency. It's not just about speaking the truth—it's about being open and sincere in your intentions. In relationships, honesty builds trust and creates authentic connection. But it must be balanced with consideration for the other person's feelings and perspective, or it risks coming across as blunt or harsh.

Compassion builds on that foundation by adding empathy and emotional understanding to communication. It's about recognizing and responding to the needs of others with kindness and care. Compassion ensures that your honesty doesn't come across as harsh by guiding you to frame your words in a way that takes the other person's emotional state into account. It strengthens connection by showing that you genuinely care about the well-being of the person you're communicating with.

Humility, like a well-built roof, caps out the trivium by encouraging openness to feedback and a willingness to acknowledge when you don't have all the answers. It allows for two-way communication, where you not only express your thoughts but also listen and learn from others. Humility fosters an environment of respect and mutual understanding, making it easier to have honest conversations while still holding onto compassion.

Together, these three elements—honesty, compassion, and humility—work in harmony to create a balanced, clear, and effective approach to communication, whether in personal relationships or professional settings.

CHAPTER ELEVEN
READ THE ROOM

Adaptive communication is about adjusting your approach to connect with others in the moment.

Adaptive communication is like a chameleon—it shifts to match its surroundings. By adjusting your communication style to fit your audience, you can avoid creating awkward situations. Up to this point, we've spent a lot of time focusing on how to respond to others, but now let's flip the perspective. When it's your turn to speak, there are key elements to keep in mind. By considering and managing these, you won't just translate what others are saying—you'll begin to speak in a way that actually connects and resonates.

Whether you're catching up with a friend, presenting in a boardroom, or writing an email, adapting your approach helps ensure your message gets through. So let's look at how to tailor your communication style to your audience, choose the right words, and adjust your tone and delivery to fit the context.

Style & Audience

Talking to people—no matter who they are or what setting you're in—means recognizing that they're more than just data processors or recorders. You're speaking to a human heart. Understanding your audience is like having a roadmap that helps you connect with those hearts. I'm not saying a CEO delivering quarterly projections should get emotional about revenue trends. What I mean is that knowing your audience means seeing them as living, breathing individuals. If you truly care about your message being heard, understood, and acted upon, you have to speak with intention—to a specific person or type of person. Focus on one, and you'll engage them all. Focus on all, and you'll lose them one by one.

So how do you do this? If you're speaking to a crowd, forget the old "picture them in their underwear" trick—I've got something better. Think about the type of person who's generally in your audience. Then, identify someone you actually know who fits that description. Once you have that person in mind, shape your message as if you're speaking directly to them. You can even use real-life examples from your relationship (with their permission, of course) to make your points more relatable. When you picture a real person as your listener, your message becomes more natural—and everyone in the room is more likely to find something that connects with them.

When you're speaking one-on-one or in a small group, focus on the main idea you want to communicate. Then, use specific examples from your relationship with that person—or those people—to help reinforce your point. If you truly care about being understood, you'll need to put in the effort to speak to a real heart, not just a set of ears. Communication isn't just about what you say—it's about what others actually hear. So take the time to shape your conversations in a way that helps people really receive your message.

This audience awareness doesn't end once you start talking. You have to make eye contact and really pay attention to people's reactions. If someone winces at something you said, pause and take stock of what just came out of your mouth. Be honest and ask a question like, "What did you hear?" I do this all the time with my wife and kids. When I notice someone responding in a way I didn't expect, I'll say, "Hold on—I feel like I'm not communicating clearly. What did you hear me say?" Almost every time I do that, I realize something was off. Maybe my tone came across as disingenuous, or maybe the words I used just didn't fit the moment. As communicators—in other words, as humans— we have to stay mindful of our audience. Whether it's your spouse or your supervisor, it's vital that you take time to understand them and pay close attention as you speak.

Breaking Ice

The hardest part of public speaking—or having difficult conversations—is often just getting started. Breaking the ice isn't just a cliché; it's the real challenge when facing awkward or uncomfortable conversations we'd rather avoid. Starting is where most people get stuck, especially when the topic is tense or significant. It's one thing to know who you need to talk to—but actually beginning that conversation can feel overwhelming. And that's often where the most important communication breaks down—the conversations we need most never happen simply because we don't know how to begin. To help with this, I've outlined several different audience types and included some examples of how to start conversations with each one.

Let's start with the hardest and work our way backward.

Hostile Audience

A hostile audience is skeptical or opposed to your message. To communicate effectively with them, acknowledge their concerns, and find common ground. Use respectful language and provide evidence to support your points. Patience and empathy are crucial.

Starter Tip: *"I understand there are some concerns about this topic. Let's address them together and find a solution that works for everyone."*

Why it Works: *This approach acknowledges their skepticism and opens the floor for a collaborative discussion.*

Distracted Audience

Distracted audiences are not fully focused on your message. Capture their attention with engaging stories, visuals, and direct questions. Keep your message concise and impactful, and try to minimize distractions in the environment.

Starter Tip: *"I have a quick story that really highlights the importance of what we're discussing today."*

Why it Works: *A captivating story grabs attention and sets the stage for your main message.*

Critical Audience

A critical audience analyzes your message in detail and may question your points. Be prepared with well-researched information and anticipate their questions. Address their concerns directly and provide clear, logical explanations to build credibility.

Starter Tip: *"I've gathered some detailed information on this topic and would love to hear your thoughts and questions."*

Why it Works: *This shows respect for their analytical approach and invites them to engage critically with your message.*

Executive Audience

Executives are often pressed for time and require high-level, results-oriented communication. Present your main points quickly and clearly, focusing on the benefits and implications of your message. Use data and examples to support your arguments, and be ready for follow-up questions.

Starter Tip: *"In just a few minutes, I'll outline the key benefits and implications of our proposal."*

Why it Works: *This respects their time constraints and sets the expectation for a concise, focused discussion.*

Generalist Audience

Generalists have a broad but not deep knowledge of many topics. Avoid overly technical language and provide a balanced overview of your message. Use analogies and relatable examples to make complex ideas more accessible.

Starter Tip: *"Think of this concept like [simple analogy]. It helps us understand [topic] in a straightforward way."*

Why it Works: *Analogies make complex ideas relatable and easier to grasp for a generalist audience.*

Expert Audience

Experts have deep knowledge in a specific field. Respect their expertise by providing detailed and accurate information. Avoid oversimplification and be prepared to dive deep into technical aspects. Engage them with challenging questions and invite their input.

Starter Tip: *"Given your expertise, I'm interested in your perspective on these detailed findings."*

Why it Works: *This respects their knowledge and invites them to contribute to a high-level discussion.*

Ideological Audience
An ideological audience holds strong beliefs that may influence their reception of your message. Recognize and respect their values, and find ways to align your message with their beliefs. Be careful not to confront their ideology directly but instead show how your message can complement their values.

Starter Tip: *"I respect the strong values you hold. Let's discuss how this idea can align with and support those values."*

Why it Works: *This acknowledges their beliefs and seeks common ground, making your message more palatable.*

Friendly Audience
A friendly audience already supports or agrees with you. Reinforce their beliefs by providing new insights and encouraging their enthusiasm. Engage them with interactive discussions and validate their opinions to maintain their support.

Starter Tip: *"I appreciate your support on this. Let's explore some new ideas that can make this even better."*

Why it Works: *This approach reinforces their existing support and opens the door for new, engaging ideas.*

Using these conversation starters can help you break the ice and connect with your audience—even when the subject is difficult. By tailoring your approach to fit the type of audience you're speaking to, you give your message a better chance of not just being heard, but truly understood.

Tone & Delivery

As we bring this chapter to a close, there are still a couple of important things to remember when you're the one doing the communicating. Your tone—the inflection and cadence of your voice—matters more than you might think. Naturally outgoing or boisterous people often rely on tone to convey meaning, but that's only a small subset of the population. For those who aren't naturally expressive, tone is a skill that must be developed with intentionality. On the flip side, those with a naturally dramatic delivery can sometimes overdo it—coming across as overwhelming or exhausting. When everything is emphasized, nothing stands out. As the old saying goes, there's a ditch on both sides of the road.

Tone is a subtle tool, but it carries a lot of power. It's not just about what you say—it's how you say it that truly shapes how your message is received. The same words can come across as supportive, neutral, or even confrontational, depending on your tone. For example, saying, "I need to talk to you," could sound like a gentle invitation or a stern warning—simply based on how it's delivered.

Both spoken and written communication rely heavily on tone. In face-to-face conversations, tone comes through in your voice and body language. In writing, it's your punctuation, word choice, and sentence structure that do the heavy lifting. Even emojis can help set the tone in more casual settings, adding a layer of emotion that text alone can't always convey.

When tone really matters, nothing beats spoken communication. Technology can either enhance or hinder clarity, depending on how it's used. If you want your listener to truly understand where you're coming from—and the message is important—resist the temptation to rely solely on written words. A phone call or video chat is often the best choice when you need to handle things quickly or from a distance. I know, making calls isn't everyone's favorite thing (it's definitely not mine), but sometimes it's necessary.

If a call doesn't feel right or you want to put more thought into what you're saying, consider sending a voice or video message instead of typing it out. Most phones have that option, and it helps ensure your tone and intent come through clearly.

Choosing the right platform for your message is key. Texts work well for quick, casual conversations but can easily lead to misunderstandings. Emails are better for detailed, formal communication, while handwritten letters offer a personal, thoughtful touch. Still, when it comes to conveying emotion or subtle nuance, nothing beats spoken communication—whether in person, over the phone, or through a voice or video message.

Face-to-face conversations are ideal for sensitive or complicated topics, where body language and other nonverbal cues play a big role. On the phone, it's all about the tone of your voice, since your listener can't see you. And if you need to share the same message with a larger group, recorded messages—especially videos—can be a great option.

One thing to keep in mind with any kind of written or recorded communication: once you send it, it's out there for good. There's no "unsending" a message that can be re-read or replayed with a critical eye. That's why, sometimes, the best approach is to have the conversation face-to-face—even if it feels uncomfortable.

Context is King

One final thought—always consider the situation you're communicating in. A serious topic calls for a respectful and measured tone, while a celebratory message can be more upbeat and informal. Pay attention to your audience's expectations, and adjust your approach to match the moment.

When you're the one communicating, adaptability is your greatest tool. Whether you're addressing a room full of people or having a one-on-one conversation, the way you present your message—your tone, your words, and the platform you choose—matters just as much as the message itself. Staying mindful of who you're speaking to and how your words will be received helps prevent misunderstandings and ensures your message truly lands. In the end, it's not just about delivering information—it's about creating connection and making sure people walk away with clarity, not confusion.

CHAPTER TWELVE
WATCH YOUR STEP

Learn to recognize and navigate the subtle pitfalls that sabotage clarity, connection, and honest communication.

There are plenty of traps that can derail positive, meaningful communication. In this final chapter, I'll highlight some of the most common ones and offer practical strategies for avoiding them. We'll move through several fairly quickly, but we'll spend more time on the two biggest culprits: ambiguity and misinterpretations— because those are the ones that tend to cause the most trouble when we're aiming for clear and honest connection.

Assumptions & Stereotypes
When it comes to communication, assumptions and stereotypes are like potholes on a road trip—they can jolt the conversation off course. Assumptions are those unchecked beliefs we carry without verifying, while stereotypes are broad generalizations that often lead to misunderstandings. To steer clear of these pitfalls, we have to notice them—and intentionally work against them.

Small Talk & Topic Avoidance
Conversations often fall into predictable patterns that limit their potential. On one side, there's the Small Talk Trap—the belief that every initial exchange must stick to surface-level topics like the weather or last night's game. While small talk can be a comfortable starting point, venturing into deeper, even sensitive topics—with care—often leads to richer and more meaningful conversations. In contrast, the Topic

Avoidance stereotype keeps people from engaging at all, out of fear that certain subjects are too controversial. Avoiding tough topics might keep things smooth, but it can also make conversations feel like a stale cracker—safe, but not very satisfying.

Agreement Fallacy & Debate Mode

Another common dichotomy is the Agreement Fallacy versus Debate Mode. The Agreement Fallacy is the belief that maintaining harmony means agreeing on everything. But the truth is, healthy disagreement can spark meaningful dialogue and lead to deeper understanding. On the other hand, Debate Mode assumes that every disagreement must turn into a heated argument. Not every differing opinion needs to become a battle. Sometimes, it's more about exploring perspectives than proving a point. Think of it like a friendly game of catch—not a dodgeball match.

The Monologue & Rushed Responses

The Monologue contrasts sharply with the Rushed Response. The Monologue Misconception is the idea that one person should dominate the conversation while others simply listen, turning the interaction into a one-sided speech. On the flip side, the Rapid Response Expectation demands immediate answers, leaving no room for thoughtful reflection. Both extremes get in the way of real dialogue. Aim for a back-and-forth exchange where everyone has a chance to share their thoughts. Remember to pause and ask, "What do you think?" And don't be afraid to say, "Let me think about that for a second." It's not a race.

Feelings Filter & Fact-Only Focus

The Feelings Filter stereotype contrasts with the Fact-Only Focus. Emotion Avoidance is the belief that emotions should be left out of serious conversations, while Fact-Only Focus dismisses personal experiences or feelings, assuming only hard facts matter. But emotions are a meaningful part of how we experience the world, and expressing them can lead to stronger, more authentic connections. Balancing facts with personal insight makes conversations more relatable and memorable. If someone seems upset, it's perfectly okay to ask, "How are you feeling about this?" alongside discussing the facts. After all, we're not robots.

Formality & Universality
Lastly, there's the Formality Trap versus the Universal Method. The Formality Trap assumes formal language is always necessary—especially in professional settings—which can create distance. On the other hand, the Universal Method assumes one communication style works for everyone, ignoring individual preferences. Balancing professionalism with a warm, approachable tone often leads to more open and productive conversations. Pay attention to cues and adjust your style accordingly— communication is more art than science.

Spotting these stereotypes is the first step to avoiding them. Remember, communication isn't just about what you say—it's also about what others actually hear. Challenge your assumptions by asking questions and taking time to understand the real nature and purpose of the conversation.

Clarifying Ambiguity

Clear communication is like a well-lit path—everyone can see where they're going. As we've seen throughout this book, honest and real communication is something many people are afraid of. The fear of awkwardness doesn't just shut conversations down—it often leaves things only half said. And while silence can stall progress, ambiguity might be even worse. When we leave room for confusion, misunderstandings creep in and derail what could have been a meaningful exchange.

Think of a conversation like a train ride. Sometimes, you can clearly tell when the train goes off the rails—maybe because of a vague statement or a misunderstood word. If you're the one speaking, watch for cues like body language, facial expressions, and verbal responses to help you catch those moments. When something seems off or the reaction doesn't match what you intended, it's time to pause and backtrack. If you're the one listening, you might need to introduce a little healthy awkwardness and politely ask for clarification. Something as simple as, "When you mentioned X, did you mean Y?" can make all the difference. The goal on either side is the same: address the ambiguity and get the conversation back on track.

When ambiguity isn't addressed head-on, misconceptions start to grow like weeds—they spread quickly and pop up everywhere. The moment you sense confusion or a misunderstanding, that's your cue to step in. If you let it linger, those weeds take root, and clearing them out later becomes much harder. It's often better to be a little blunt upfront to make sure your message is clear. For example, you might say, "I want to make sure I was clear earlier—what I meant was..." That kind of proactive approach cuts off confusion before it spreads. Addressing misconceptions early keeps people from building entire scenarios around a message you didn't mean to send—and that saves everyone a lot of unnecessary frustration.

Another helpful strategy is to ask open-ended questions. These types of questions go beyond a simple yes or no and invite the other person to elaborate. Instead of asking, "Did you mean X?" try, "Can you tell me more about what you meant by X?" That extra space gives them a chance to clarify, which can reveal where the communication may have gone off track. After covering a particularly complex point—or once you've made it through a lot of ground—it's smart to summarize what's been said and reflect it back. Something as simple as, "So, if I understand you correctly, you're saying that…" gives them the opportunity to confirm or correct your understanding. It's a practical way to make sure you're both on the same page before moving forward.

When you're trying to clarify ambiguous messages, simplicity is your best friend. Use clear, straightforward language to get your point across. Avoid jargon or overly complex words that only add to the confusion. Sure, we all want to sound intelligent and articulate—but the real goal is to make your message easy to understand. Clarity takes patience and openness. Sometimes people just need a moment to gather their thoughts or find the right words, and giving them that space can make all the difference.

Managing Misinterpretations

Misinterpretations are bound to happen, but with a little patience and the right approach, you can clear them up and keep the conversation moving forward. Here are two simple methods I've found helpful for untangling those moments of confusion.

Detangling Wires

This one takes some practice, but it's worth the effort. Picture trying to untangle a mess of wires—you have to trace each one back to its knot and gently work it loose. Conversations aren't much different. When things get tangled, our instinct is to push through, hoping it'll sort itself out. That might work with wires now and then, but it doesn't work with people. In fact, trying to force it usually makes things worse.

Start by acknowledging the misunderstanding: "I realize there was a mix-up earlier." That simple step shows you're aware and willing to work through it together. Then, walk through the conversation one step at a time. Pinpoint where things went off track, and clarify what you really meant. For example, "When I said X, I meant Y." Be clear, but stay gentle—make sure the other person feels heard, not blamed. A simple question like, "What did you take from that?" can open the door for them to share their perspective.

Even after you think things are cleared up, there might still be a few lingering misunderstandings. Keep the conversation open, and let them know you're available to circle back if needed. You're both human—it takes time to fully work through these things. Staying open to continued dialogue helps those corrections settle in and stick.

Work Together
Once you've worked through the misunderstanding, it's important to re-establish mutual understanding. Invite the other person to ask questions or share feedback—something as simple as, "Let's go over this again to make sure we're on the same page." That kind of invitation shows you value their input and care about clarity on both sides. Active listening is key here. Pay close attention to what they're saying, and be genuinely empathetic to how they're feeling.

Sometimes people need to voice their frustration or confusion before they're ready to accept the clarified information—so stay calm and give them space. Depending on the situation, things like visual aids or a quick written summary can help reinforce your points. For more complex topics, it's often helpful to highlight key takeaways and follow up with another conversation or even a short email to make sure everything lands the way it should.

Working together to clear things up doesn't just fix the moment—it strengthens your overall communication for whatever comes next. This kind of collaboration builds trust and deepens understanding, making conversations smoother down the road. And just like a broken bone often heals stronger, a conversation that's been repaired well can lead to even better connection than before.

CONCLUSION

You don't have to be a natural speaker, a master persuader, or some social genius to communicate well—you just have to be willing. Willing to practice. Willing to lean in. Willing to be honest, compassionate, and humble. The awkward moments you've feared aren't roadblocks—they're invitations to grow.

Communication isn't just a skill; it's a responsibility. Every conversation you have shapes your relationships and your influence. So don't coast. Don't settle for shallow exchanges and half-said truths. Step into the awkward, speak with intention, and keep sharpening your ability to connect. You're not done learning—none of us are. But you're further along than you were when you started. The real work starts now—so speak like it matters.

ABOUT THE AUTHOR

Josh is a pastor, coach, and communicator with a passion for helping people grow through life's most uncomfortable moments. With nearly two decades of pastoral ministry experience and a background in leadership roles across both nonprofit and startup sectors, Josh brings a unique blend of wisdom, clarity, and practical insight to the subject of communication.

He is the author of Awkward Communication: Mastering Communication Through Life's Uncomfortable Moments, the first in a series designed to help readers navigate everyday conversations with confidence, humility, and purpose.

Known for his straightforward, relatable style, Josh's writing bridges the gap between timeless truth and real-world application. Whether he's preaching, coaching, or writing, his goal is the same: to equip others to speak with boldness, listen with grace, and connect with deeper intentionality.

A native Floridian, Josh is in management in the manufacturing sector while also devoting himself to writing, coaching, and preaching. He's a committed family man who enjoys life's adventures with his wife, Sarah, and their two children.

www.ingramcontent.com/pod-product-compliance
Lightning Source LLC
Chambersburg PA
CBHW070538030426
42337CB00016B/2249